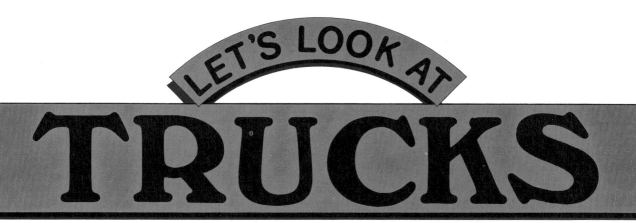

LET'S LOOK AT TRUCKS

Andrew Langley

Language Consultant
Diana Bentley
University of Reading

Artist
Peter Gregory

Let's Look At

Bikes

Castles

Colours

Dinosaurs

Farming

Horses

Outer Space

Rain

Sunshine

The Seasons

Tractors

Trucks

Editors: Rhoda Nottridge & Elizabeth Spiers

First published in 1988 by
Wayland (Publishers) Ltd
61 Western Road, Hove
East Sussex BN3 1JD, England

© Copyright Wayland (Publishers) Ltd

British Library Cataloguing in Publication Data
Langley, Andrew
    Let's look at trucks.
    1. Lorries – For children
    I. Title   II. Gregory, Peter, *1947–*
    629.2′24

    ISBN 1–85210–481–3

Phototypeset by Kalligraphics Ltd, Horley, Surrey
Printed and bound by Casterman, S.A., Belgium

Words printed in
bold are explained
in the glossary.

Contents

Giants of the road

Trucks are the biggest and strongest vehicles on the road. They can carry heavy loads a long way. Some big trucks have special jobs to do, such as clearing snow.

Not all trucks are giants. There are small vans, delivering letters and milk from door to door. There are also farm trucks, which take crops or animals to market. Between them, trucks help to carry nearly everything we eat or wear or use.

The first trucks

The first powered truck was built in France 200 years ago. It had a **steam engine** and only three wheels. But it did not last very long. On its first trip, the steam truck crashed into a wall!

Later on, trucks were made with **petrol engines**. Soon petrol-driven trucks replaced the old steam trucks. They could travel much faster and were cheaper to run. They were also lighter, so they did not damage the roads.

Today's trucks

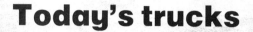

This is a modern truck. It is made in two parts. The front part is called the tractor. This carries the powerful engine and the fuel tank. The engine uses **diesel fuel**. On top is the cab where the driver sits. The truck has strong brakes and more than twenty **gears** to help it go up steep hills with a heavy load.

Behind the tractor is the **trailer**, where the cargo is stored. The wheels have wide tyres that give a good grip on the road.

Door to door

Every day the city streets are full of trucks. They are delivering all kinds of goods. Some are taking groceries to the shops. Some are carrying furniture and clothes. Special strong trucks take money to the banks. Dust carts are collecting rubbish.

Most delivery trucks are loaded at **warehouses** or factories. Some have a lift platform at the back. The cargo is placed on the platform, and an electric motor raises the platform so it is level with the back of the truck.

Long distance

Trucks may carry loads over very long distances. Some even travel right across Europe, North America or Australia. They deliver their trailers and then pick up another to take back.

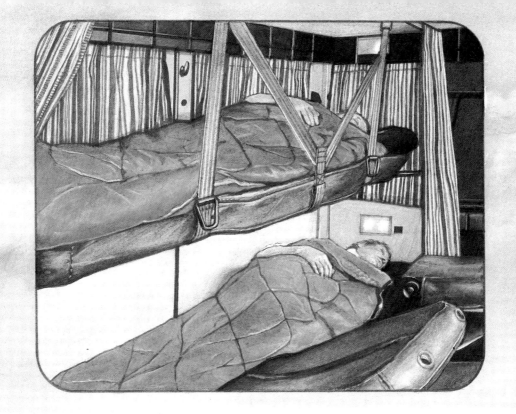

Long distance drivers can live in their trucks for many days. Most cabs are like tiny travelling homes. Behind the driving seat is a bed, a wash-basin and perhaps a television. At night the driver pulls curtains over the windscreen and goes to sleep in his cab.

13

Tankers

A tanker is a truck with a large tank on the back. Tankers carry goods such as liquids and gases which cannot be loaded in the normal way. The tanks are sealed tightly so that none of the load can escape.

Some tankers carry petrol or other chemicals which can easily catch fire or explode. The drivers must be very careful. But most tankers carry goods such as milk, which are not dangerous at all.

Containers

Today many goods are loaded into big boxes called containers. A crane lifts the full container on to the back of a truck. The truck is driven to the port, where the container is lifted off and put on to a boat. Containers can also be sent by rail.

Goods can be moved more cheaply and quickly by containers than by ordinary trucks. They do not have to be loaded and unloaded bit by bit.

Army trucks

One of the biggest army trucks is the British M2 transporter. It can travel across land or water. Several M2s can be joined together to form an instant bridge.

Soldiers need trucks for all sorts of jobs. They are used to carry troops and supplies, or to pull heavy guns. Huge **transporters** carry battle tanks over long distances. Some trucks are used as launching pads for firing **missiles**. Others carry vital radio equipment.

Emergency!

There's a fire! Special fire engines race to the scene. They are another kind of truck. Some of them pump water and foam on to the flames. Another truck has a long turntable ladder. This is used to rescue people trapped high up by the fire.

Did you know that an ambulance is also a special kind of truck for carrying sick people to hospital? In an emergency, the ambulance speeds through the streets. Its sirens and flashing blue lights warn people to get out of the way.

Fire engines also help at traffic accidents. They carry equipment for cutting up wrecked vehicles.

Road trains

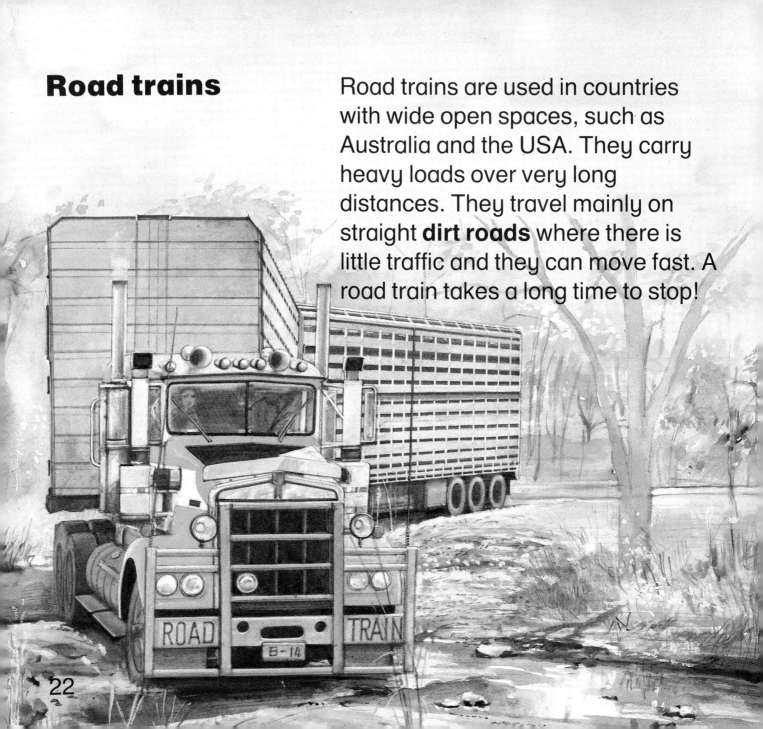

Road trains are used in countries with wide open spaces, such as Australia and the USA. They carry heavy loads over very long distances. They travel mainly on straight **dirt roads** where there is little traffic and they can move fast. A road train takes a long time to stop!

They have a tractor in the front and several huge trailers behind. As you can see from this truck in Saudi Arabia, there is a loud horn on top of the cab to tell people that the road train is coming.

Earth movers

When a new road is built, mountains of earth and rock must be moved. This is done by giant tipper trucks. The trucks are filled with **rubble**. They carry it away from the site and tip it where it is needed. Some tippers can carry180 tonnes. Their huge tyres are over 3 metres high.

24

Much smaller tippers are used on building sites all over the world. They are called dumper trucks. They carry earth, bricks, timber or cement to where it is needed on the site.

Building trucks

The engine, tyres and other parts of a truck are made in separate factories. They may even be made in different countries. The parts are all sent to an **assembly plant** where they are put together.

In some plants the assembly work is done by **robots**. The robots control machines. Some join the metal parts together. Others spray paint on to the new truck. When the truck is finished, it is carefully inspected to make sure that it has no faults.

Record breakers

The biggest truck in the world is called the Crawler. This huge transporter carries the **Space Shuttle** to its launch pad at Cape Canaveral in the USA. The Crawler weighs 3,000 tonnes and its top speed is 3 kilometres per hour.

The fastest fire truck is the Jaguar, built in 1982. It has a top speed of 210 kilometres per hour.

The biggest dumper truck in the world is the American Titan. When fully loaded, it weighs 548 tonnes.

The longest ever truck is the Snow Train, built in Texas, USA. It stretches for more than 174 metres and has 54 wheels.

American Titan

Glossary

Assembly plant   A factory where the different parts of a truck or car are put together.

Diesel fuel   A heavy oil, based on petrol, which is used to fire a diesel engine. Most trucks have diesel engines.

Dirt roads   Roads that have not been given a proper hard surface. They are covered with bare earth or rubble.

Gears   A set of toothed wheels that enable the driver to change speed or direction.

Missiles   Weapons that are thrown from a base and land on an enemy target.

Petrol engines   Engines that are fired by petrol.

Robot   A machine that works automatically or by remote control.

Rubble   Pieces of rock and soil dug up during building or mining work.

Sirens   Instruments that make a wailing or whistling noise as a signal or warning.

Space Shuttle   A spacecraft that is able to make repeated journeys in space.

Steam engine   An engine that makes use of the power of steam under pressure.

Trailer   A large wagon for carrying cargo, which is hauled by a tractor.

Transporter   A large truck that carries very heavy loads, especially other vehicles such as tanks and diggers.

Warehouse   A large building where goods are stored before being sold.

Books to read

Big Trucks, Michael Jay (Franklin Watts, 1986)

Looking at Trucks, Cliff Lines (Wayland, 1984)

The Lorry Driver, Anne Stewart (Hamish Hamilton, 1985)

Trucks, Norman Barrett (Franklin Watts, 1986)

Trucks, Ian Ottley (Hodder & Stoughton, 1984)

What About Trucks, Ron Joyce Cave (Franklin Watts, 1982)

Index